Who Is Queen Elizabeth II?

by Megan Stine

illustrated by Laurie A. Conley

Penguin Workshop

For Bill, who visited Buckingham Palace with me
and loves his afternoon tea—MS

For my family and our Canadian roots—LAC

PENGUIN WORKSHOP
An Imprint of Penguin Random House LLC, New York

Copyright © 2021 by Penguin Random House LLC. All rights reserved.
Published by Penguin Workshop, an imprint of Penguin Random House LLC, New York.
PENGUIN and PENGUIN WORKSHOP are trademarks of Penguin Books Ltd.
WHO HQ & Design is a registered trademark of Penguin Random House LLC.
Printed in the USA.

Visit us online at www.penguinrandomhouse.com.

Library of Congress Cataloging-in-Publication Data is available upon request.

ISBN 9780593097519 (paperback)   10 9 8 7 6 5 4 3 2 1 WOR
ISBN 9780593097526 (library binding)   10 9 8 7 6 5 4 3 2 1 WOR

Contents

Who Is Queen Elizabeth II?

Ten-year-old Princess Elizabeth had spent time in castles and palaces in England and Scotland since she'd been born. Her father was a duke. Her grandfather was the king of the United Kingdom, or the UK, which included England, Scotland, Wales, and Northern Ireland. Like a fairy-tale princess, Elizabeth led a happy, carefree life in a big house in London.

Called Lilibet by family members, Elizabeth had everything a princess could want—dogs, ponies, tiaras, closets full of pretty dresses, and a lot of free time. She didn't go to school. She was taught by her nanny at home. At the age of six, she was given her own tiny cottage with a thatched roof made of straw. It was a playhouse for her and her younger sister, Margaret. It came with a working kitchen and child-sized furniture in all the rooms.

Lilibet and Margaret were incredibly popular with the British people. Even as a baby, Lilibet received letters and gifts—three tons of toys!—from people as far away as Australia.

Although Elizabeth was a princess, she never expected to become a queen herself.

Her uncle Edward was the oldest son of the king, so he was first in line for the throne. Lilibet's father, Albert, was second in line. That meant Edward would become king after his father died. Once Edward had children of his own, his oldest child would be second in line. Lilibet's father would move down the list, and probably never become king.

And at first, when Lilibet's grandfather died in January 1936, that's what happened. Her uncle became King Edward VIII.

But later that year, everything changed.

Edward had fallen in love with an American woman. He wanted to marry her. But she had been divorced—twice. According to the Church of England, a king could not marry a divorced woman. Edward wanted to marry her so much, he decided to give up being king.

King Edward VIII

On December 10, 1936, King Edward VIII abdicated—he gave up the throne. He signed papers and immediately stepped down. When he did that, Lilibet's father instantly became the king. Her father's real name was Albert, but he chose George as his royal name: King George VI. Now that her father was king, Lilibet was suddenly next in line for the throne!

King George VI and his wife, Queen Elizabeth

A servant came to tell Elizabeth the news. He bowed as he entered the room. From that moment on, everyone treated her differently, and her life was planned out for her. She had only one job— learning how to become a queen.

One day, she would rule over an empire that included fifty-four countries around the world. At the age of ten, Elizabeth had no idea how quickly that might happen.

CHAPTER 1
A Young Princess

Elizabeth Alexandra Mary Windsor was born at home on a rainy night, April 21, 1926. While Lilibet was a baby, her family moved to an enormous house in London. It had a

ballroom, a library, and twenty-five bedrooms.

Once her father was king, her family moved into Buckingham Palace—an enormous palace in the center of London. It had 775 rooms with hundreds of people working there. Huge iron gates at the front kept people out. So did guards dressed in bright red uniforms including tall bearskin hats.

Lilibet's father had never wanted to be king. King George VI was shy and stuttered when he spoke. He loved horses and dogs. When Lilibet was only three, she had her first riding lesson. When she was seven, her father gave her a Welsh corgi named Dookie. From then on, she loved horses and corgis—almost more than anything else.

Lilibet's nanny was named Marion Crawford. Everyone called her Crawfie. She spent nearly all day with Lilibet and Margaret, teaching them

history, reading, geography, and grammar.

As a young child, Lilibet was sometimes naughty. She had a hot temper like her father and grandfather. But as Elizabeth grew up, her mother taught her to control her anger. She told her never to shout at people—especially when she became queen—or people would lose their trust in her.

By the time she was ten, Lilibet had turned into a serious girl. She liked to have fun with her family and could be friendly and charming. But she was quiet and dignified in public. She already knew how to act like a queen.

Lilibet's younger sister, Margaret, was the opposite of her—wild and free. She loved mocking the way famous people spoke. Lilibet laughed but would never do anything like that herself.

Elizabeth's father once said, "Lilibet is my pride. Margaret is my joy." Both girls visited their parents' bedroom every morning to play and have fun. It was a family tradition.

How the British Government Works

The system of having kings and queens is called a monarchy. At one time, British monarchs had total power to rule. But today, the king or queen holds almost no power.

The government in the United Kingdom is called Parliament. Members of Parliament make the laws,

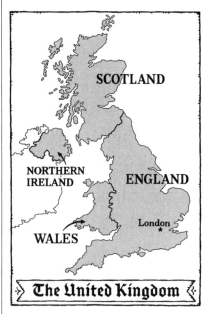

and the monarch is expected to agree to them. This system is called a constitutional monarchy.

There are two separate branches of Parliament: the House of Lords and the House of Commons.

The House of Lords includes religious leaders, dukes, duchesses, and other members of British nobility. Some are elected, but most are allowed to sit in the House of Lords just because of their titles.

The House of Commons is different. Men and women are elected by the public from all over the United Kingdom. The leader of the House of Commons is the prime minister. That job is similar to being the president in the United States.

Elizabeth in the Girl Guides

Sometimes, Crawfie and the young princesses left Buckingham Palace for a day so they could see what ordinary life was like. The nanny also started a Girl Guides troop in the palace. The Girl Guides are like the Girl Scouts in the United States. Still, all of Lilibet's playmates and friends had to curtsy to her and call her Ma'am because she would be queen one day.

When Lilibet turned thirteen, she started studying with a tutor named Sir Henry Marten.

Twice a week, Lilibet went to Marten's study, where he kept a pet raven. Marten taught Lilibet all about the rules and laws of the country. It was a lot to learn—but Lilibet needed to know all of it. She would need to understand exactly what she could and couldn't do as the monarch.

Lilibet didn't mind all the studying required of her. But she did mind having to live cooped up in Buckingham Palace. She spent hours at the windows, looking out at the world and wondering what a normal life would be like.

At night, the young princess knelt beside her bed and said her prayers. Her mother was very religious, and Lilibet was, too. In England, the monarch is the head of the Church of England. One day, Lilibet would become head of the church.

As she grew up, Lilibet learned how to behave properly in public. Her mother taught her to sit up so straight that her back never touched the back of a chair. She learned that she should never cry in public—even if she fell down or hurt herself. Lilibet's grandmother, Queen Mary, told her that a queen should never smile in public! Lilibet and Margaret always had to curtsy to their grandmother.

After World War II broke out in Europe in 1939, German planes dropped thousands of bombs on London. Buckingham Palace was bombed nine times. Lilibet's parents, the king and queen, didn't flee the city, though. They stayed in the palace to show the country that they were facing dangers like everyone else. But Lilibet and Margaret were sent to live in Windsor Castle, twenty miles away.

World War II

World War II started on September 1, 1939, when Germany invaded Poland. Great Britain and France declared war on Germany two days later. Germany was led by Adolf Hitler, who wanted to take over Europe. From 1940 to 1941, the Germans

dropped bombs on London, destroying many buildings. The bombing was called "the Blitz," and at one point, it went on for fifty-seven nights in a row. Tens of thousands of people were injured or killed. Germany was defeated in 1945 by a group of countries led by the United States, Great Britain, and the Soviet Union.

At Windsor Castle, Elizabeth and Margaret spent a lot of time with young soldiers who were there to protect them. Crawfie invented games for the girls and soldiers to play—treasure hunts and versions of hide-and-seek. At Christmas, Elizabeth performed in a show at the castle. She sang and tap-danced for the soldiers and townspeople.

The war years at Windsor Castle weren't all fun and games, though. Life there was hard. The whistling sounds of bombs falling filled the night air. Even the royal family had to do without some basic necessities. They had very little hot water. Bathtubs were filled to only five inches deep. When the bombing was bad in London, the king and queen would retreat to Windsor Castle at night. They slept with Elizabeth and Margaret in a shelter under one of the castle towers.

At eighteen, Elizabeth was old enough to

help with the war effort. She spent three weeks in the women's branch of the army, in England. She learned how to drive a truck, change spark plugs, and fix the truck's engine. She later said it was the only time she had the chance to compare herself with other people her age.

The British people loved seeing photos of their favorite princess in uniform. Everyone wanted to defeat the Nazis. The war taught Elizabeth how important it was for the whole country to pull together—and for the royal family to do its part in making that happen.

CHAPTER 2
Royal Wedding

Something else was happening during the war years. Elizabeth was falling in love.

The young man she fell in love with was a navy officer. He was five years older than she was. But he wasn't just a navy officer. He was her third cousin and a prince—Prince Philip of Greece and Denmark.

Like many people in Europe's royal families, Philip was related to a lot of kings and queens. He and Elizabeth had the same great-great-grandparents—Queen Victoria and Prince Albert. In those days, it was common for royal cousins to marry each other.

Thirteen-year-old Elizabeth fell in love with Philip almost from the moment she saw him.

Prince Philip

He was six feet tall with blue eyes and blond hair—athletic, witty, and handsome. Truly a prince charming! But he wasn't rich.

Elizabeth's mother thought she should marry someone else—someone with money and land. But Elizabeth had her heart set on Philip. As Elizabeth got older, Philip fell in love with her, too. He joined the Royal Navy in 1939 and sailed around the world during World War II. But he wrote letters to her while he was gone.

In the fall of 1946, the king and queen invited Philip to spend a month with them at their favorite castle in Scotland—Balmoral. Surrounded by fifty thousand acres of beautiful woods and rolling land, it was the place Elizabeth's family went every summer. There, Philip proposed to Elizabeth, and she instantly said yes. She was twenty years old. She didn't even ask her parents for permission, although princesses were supposed to.

Her father, the king, insisted that Elizabeth keep the engagement secret until she turned twenty-one the following year. During that time, he taught Elizabeth how to be queen of the whole British Commonwealth.

On her twenty-first birthday, Elizabeth and her parents and sister were in South Africa. To celebrate, a huge ball was held in her honor, complete with fireworks. The day was declared a national holiday. The prime minister of South Africa gave her a necklace with twenty-one diamonds in it.

A few months later, her engagement to Prince Philip was announced.

The royal wedding for Elizabeth and Philip was held on November 20, 1947. By that time, Philip had given up being Prince of Greece and Denmark. Instead, he was now the Duke of Edinburgh. (Edinburgh is the capital of Scotland, which is part of the United Kingdom.)

It was freezing cold on the morning of the wedding. But that didn't stop thousands of people from crowding the streets outside Westminster

Abbey, the most famous church in England. The British people were thrilled to celebrate this beautiful new beginning after the long, terrible years of the war.

Elizabeth and her father rode to the church in a gold, black, and red horse-drawn coach—like in a fairy tale. Her dress was covered with crystals and pearls. The train for her dress was fifteen feet long!

Westminster Abbey was filled with two thousand guests. The women wore long gowns and gloves. There were more than a dozen kings, queens, and princes there.

After the ceremony, Elizabeth and Philip rode

back to Buckingham Palace in a glass coach. A hundred thousand people stood outside the palace, waiting. Finally, the royal couple arrived, appeared on the balcony of the palace, and waved to the crowds.

The British Empire and the Commonwealth

Hundreds of years ago, England sent ships all over the world to claim land for the king. At first, all the colonies and territories were part of what was called the British Empire. Britain ruled them.

New York

Maine:
Part of Massachusetts

New Hampshire

Massachusetts

Rhode Island

Connecticut

Pennsylvania

New Jersey

Virginia

Delaware

Maryland

North Carolina

South Carolina

Georgia

---- Borders
in 1775

The thirteen original colonies

Over time, though, some of the colonies became independent countries. In North America, the thirteen colonies became the United States. Still, many countries wanted to keep a connection to England—and wanted the British monarch to be their king or queen. Today, this group of fifty-four nations is called the Commonwealth of Nations. It includes Canada, Australia, Singapore, Rwanda, South Africa, and many more.

Back inside, Elizabeth and Philip cut their wedding cake with his sword. The cake was nine feet tall!

The early years of Elizabeth and Philip's marriage were happy ones. Elizabeth gave birth to her first child, Prince Charles, on November 14, 1948. The whole family was there to celebrate. The prime minister—the leader of the British government—was there, too! As Elizabeth's first child, Prince Charles was in line to be king of the United Kingdom someday.

A year later, Philip was sent by the navy to Malta, a small island country in the Mediterranean. Elizabeth decided to join him, leaving their one-year-old son behind. She wanted to spend as much time as she could with Philip. In 1950, their second child was born—Princess Anne. Elizabeth wasn't a cold mother, but she wasn't warm and cuddly with her children, either. Both Charles and Anne were cared for by nannies in London.

Prince Charles and Princess Anne

They spent Christmas with their grandparents while Elizabeth and Philip were away.

Years later, Charles would say that he felt sad as a child because his mother was gone so much. When returning from long trips, sometimes she didn't even hug him.

Meanwhile, Elizabeth's father, King George VI, was ill. He had planned to travel the world for six months to visit Commonwealth countries. But he was too weak. So he decided to send Elizabeth and Philip instead.

On January 31, 1952, Elizabeth and Philip flew to Kenya, in Africa. It was supposed to be their first stop of many. They spent a night at Treetops—a hotel built high up in the African trees. Elephants roamed below, and Elizabeth took movies of them.

While she and Philip were sleeping, Elizabeth's father—who was miles away in England—suddenly died in his sleep. It was February 6, 1952. Elizabeth was now queen. At age twenty-five, she was the monarch of England, Scotland, Wales, Northern Ireland, and dozens of other countries and territories around the world. She had never expected to become queen so young—but she was ready.

Queen Elizabeth I

The first Queen Elizabeth was crowned in 1558. During her long reign over England (1558–1603), "Good Queen Bess" was greatly loved by the people. She had a great deal of power. But over the centuries, the British monarch had less and less power. Eventually, a monarch could no longer make laws or command people to obey her or him.

CHAPTER 3
Long Live the Queen

Elizabeth and Philip immediately flew home to England, where the prime minister and other members of the government met them at the airport. They all bowed to Elizabeth, as the new Queen of the United Kingdom. At home that night, her grandmother, Queen Mary, curtsied to her and kissed her hand. It had always been the other way around!

The next day, Elizabeth took a solemn oath in front of several hundred people from the government. In a short speech, she promised to work as hard as her father had for the happiness of her people. Although she was never supposed to cry in public, her eyes were filled with tears by the time she was done.

Elizabeth was already queen, but she still had to go through the ceremony called the coronation. During the ceremony, the crown would actually be placed on her head. But that wouldn't happen for sixteen months. Why? To give everyone time to mourn the dead king before holding a joyous celebration for the new monarch.

The funeral for King George VI lasted several days. Three hundred thousand people filed past his coffin in the parliament building to pay their respects. On the day of the burial, Elizabeth rode with her mother and sister in a carriage behind the coach carrying the coffin. All three wore long, heavy black veils. The coffin was taken through London to Windsor Castle for burial.

When the funeral was over, Elizabeth had to start work as the new queen. To her surprise, she immediately felt confident in her job. She felt like a queen right away.

Every single day except Christmas Day and Easter Sunday, the young Queen had to read important papers that were brought to her in a locked red-leather box. The papers told her what was going on in Parliament.

Every week, she met with the prime minister for about half an hour. The Queen isn't supposed to tell the government what to do. She is supposed to offer advice without being too pushy. Over time, Elizabeth has become especially good at this. She asks questions that make prime ministers think hard about what Parliament should do.

Elizabeth's first prime minister was Winston Churchill. He was a famous and beloved world leader who was more than fifty-three years older than Elizabeth. He had led the country through World War II to victory. Elizabeth has had thirteen more prime ministers during her long reign, but Churchill remains her favorite.

Winston Churchill

When Elizabeth became queen, an important question came up. What would her last name be? Women usually took their husbands' last names in those days. Philip's was *Mountbatten.* But Elizabeth's mother told her to keep her family's last name—*Windsor.* Philip never really got over her decision to do so.

The Queen's daily life inside Buckingham Palace soon fell into a routine. At 9:00 a.m. each morning, she woke up to the sound of bagpipes playing under her bedroom window. She had breakfast in her bedroom, brought by servants of course.

There were also housemaids, footmen, private secretaries, and others to assist with daily chores. For special events, her ladies-in-waiting were on hand. Ladies-in-waiting aren't servants—they are close friends or cousins. They often go with the Queen when she is out in public. If she needs something, she just stares right at them, and they rush to help.

Royal Palaces and Castles

There are twenty royal palaces and castles throughout the United Kingdom. They are not only homes for royalty. They are also used as offices and for big events such as balls and large dinners. Buckingham Palace is often thought of as the Queen's home. But to Queen Elizabeth II, it is more of an office. She goes there when she is working—meeting with the prime minister or greeting heads of other countries. But she considers Windsor Castle in nearby Windsor to be her real home.

When Elizabeth was in London, she usually saw her children twice a day. The Queen played with them for a few minutes in the morning. Then they came to visit her in the late afternoon, at teatime. After tea, sometimes, she helped get them ready for bed.

Elizabeth is a kind person, but she had been brought up to believe that her first job was as queen. Every other role was less important—including being a mother.

At long last, Elizabeth's coronation was held on June 2, 1953. She had practiced every part of the ceremony for weeks. She had to wear a heavy robe with a twenty-one-foot-long train while walking down the aisle in Westminster Abbey. Her robes weighed thirty-six pounds—as much as a small child! So she rehearsed in a ballroom of the palace with sheets that were weighted down and tied to her shoulders. She also practiced wearing the heavy crown. It weighed five pounds.

Most of the ceremony was shown on TV. Millions of people watched around the world. It was the first time the public had seen a coronation. The day was cold and rainy, but a million people watched the Queen go by on her way to church. Elizabeth rode in a gold coach. Parades of soldiers and bands marched by. Six maids of honor waited for her at the church door.

Inside Westminster Abbey, the coronation was performed by the archbishop of Canterbury, the very highest religious leader in the Church of England. For one part of the ceremony, Elizabeth's maids of honor removed her robes, gloves, and jewelry. They helped her put on a plain white linen dress, over her jewel-encrusted gown. This was the most sacred part of the coronation. TV cameras were not allowed to show it. The archbishop of Canterbury poured holy oil on her palms, head, and heart. It was a way of announcing that she was then holy.

With her coronation robes back on, Elizabeth sat on a wooden throne. She was handed the crown jewels—a jeweled scepter, sword, gold ball, and ring. The scepter is a long gold stick with hundreds of diamonds, including the largest clear-cut diamond in the world. The gold ball has a cross on top. The jewels were heavy, but Elizabeth held them all perfectly.

Finally, the solid gold Saint Edward's Crown was placed on her head. It was the only time she would ever wear it. The crown was only for coronations. At the same time, all the members of nobility in the church put smaller crowns on their own heads. Then everyone cried out: "God Save the Queen!"

The coronation lasted nearly three hours. When it was over, the Queen took off the Saint Edward's Crown and put on a different one. Then she rode through the streets of London so the people could see her.

Back at the palace, the Queen was joyful. "Nothing went wrong!" she said happily.

When she took off her crown, five-year-old Charles put it on his head. The Queen didn't mind. After all, he would be wearing it himself one day.

CHAPTER 4
Country First, Family Second

Several months after the coronation, the Queen and Prince Philip left England for the first of many trips to visit countries in the British Commonwealth. She would be away nearly six months.

For her first global tour, Elizabeth had one hundred new outfits made. Most of her dresses had weights in the hem, so her skirt wouldn't blow up in the wind. She wore bright colors so people could pick her out in a crowd. She was enormously popular, wherever she went. Philip tried to keep things fun by making jokes.

But the trips were also hard work. In foreign countries, Elizabeth had to be polite and eat local food, even if she didn't like it.

On the island of Fiji, she was offered a special drink. It was made with kava—and spit! She politely took a small sip.

At the end of the trip, Elizabeth and Philip went to Libya. They were met there by a brand-new ship called *Britannia*. The Queen and Prince Philip had designed it themselves. It had a grand staircase, fancy dining room, beautifully decorated living rooms, bedrooms, and more. It was like a floating mansion.

Britannia

The whole time Elizabeth was gone, her young children had been back in England with their nannies and grandmother—alone again at Christmas.

But then, Prince Charles and Princess Anne sailed to Libya on *Britannia* to meet their parents. It was the first time seeing their mother in so long! But when Elizabeth stepped on board and saw Charles waiting to shake hands with her, she said, "No, not you, dear." She wouldn't even shake her son's hand until she had greeted the more important adults. Elizabeth felt duty to her country always came first. Family was second.

The Queen chose duty over family in another matter, too. Princess Margaret wanted to marry a man named Peter Townsend. But he was divorced.

By law, Margaret wasn't allowed to get married without the Queen's permission.

Elizabeth was strongly against divorce. She didn't want to say yes to her sister—but she didn't want to say no. So she put off giving Margaret an answer.

Finally, Margaret was told she could marry Peter Townsend—but only if she gave up the right to ever become queen. She would also have to give up the money that royal family members receive.

In the end, Margaret decided to give up Peter Townsend. She wasn't happy about it, though. Margaret had always been a bit wild. She became even harder to control.

But Elizabeth didn't let her sister upset her. No matter what happened with her family, she stayed focused on the one job she had been raised to do.

She was the Queen of England, and she planned to be a queen everyone could admire.

CHAPTER 5
Around the World

Over the next ten years, Elizabeth met with the most powerful leaders in the world. She lived through the Cold War—a time when the United States and the Soviet Union were enemies. No actual battles were fought, but everyone feared that one side might drop a nuclear bomb.

In 1956, Nikita Khrushchev, the leader of the Soviet Union, visited the United Kingdom. Elizabeth invited him to Windsor Castle and served him tea in a glass, the way Russians liked to drink it.

Nikita Khrushchev

The next year, the

Queen and Prince Philip were invited to meet US president Dwight D. Eisenhower at the White House. A fancy state dinner was held for her. (A "state dinner" is a grand dinner party held in honor of a visiting leader of a country.)

The Queen and Prince Philip with the Eisenhowers, 1957

Elizabeth wanted to see how ordinary Americans lived. She asked to attend a football game and to visit an American supermarket. The grocery stores in America were so much larger than the ones in her country. Shoppers were amazed when the Queen of England suddenly appeared in aisle six! And Elizabeth was amazed by the many things sold in the gigantic store. She had never seen frozen chicken potpies before.

In 1961, Queen Elizabeth met the next US president, John F. Kennedy, and also his wife, Jacqueline. The Queen was deeply shocked when he was assassinated in November 1963. She held a memorial service for the young president at Windsor Castle. She also made a very special gift to America—an acre of British land given to the United States forever. A stone marker was placed on the spot, honoring President Kennedy.

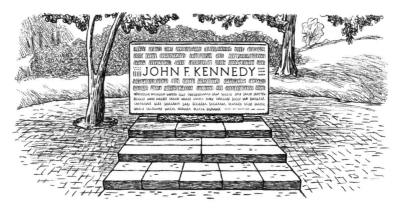

By 1964, London was the center of the rock music world. The Beatles and the Rolling Stones were superstars. The Queen didn't like rock music, but she wanted to keep up with the times.

The Beatles with their MBE medals, 1965

So in 1965, she awarded a medal to each of the four Beatles. Some people thought it was a mistake to honor the band with the same award given to war heroes.

In 1960, the Queen had her third child Prince Andrew. Prince Edward, her fourth and last child, was born on March 10, 1964. Now that she was more settled in her role as Queen, she had time to enjoy her children more. Princes

Andrew and Edward had happier childhoods. Elizabeth spent more time with them than she had with Prince Charles and Princess Anne.

Elizabeth with Philip and their children, 1965

In 1965, the Queen resumed her frequent world tours to Commonwealth nations. But South Africa was not among them. It was in turmoil because of apartheid. South Africa had decided to leave the Commonwealth in 1961.

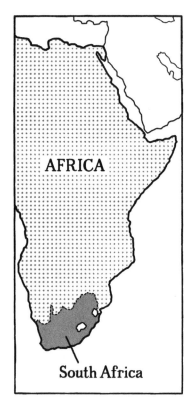

AFRICA

South Africa

Queen Elizabeth II was no longer its queen— and they wouldn't be giving her a diamond necklace again anytime soon.

While Elizabeth was tending to world affairs, who was taking care of family matters? Prince Philip was in charge. And not all the children were happy with the decisions their father made.

South Africa and Apartheid

As a British colony, South Africa had been ruled by white people even though nearly all the population was Black. In 1950, laws were passed to keep Black people separate—or apart—from whites. These laws were called apartheid. In 1961, South Africa gained its independence from the British Commonwealth, but white people continued to rule. Apartheid ended in the 1990s when Blacks were allowed to vote in the national election. In 1994, Nelson Mandela became the country's first Black president.

Nelson Mandela

CHAPTER 6
Charles's Unhappy Childhood

When Charles was only eight years old, the Queen and Prince Philip decided to send their son to live and study away from home at a boarding school. Philip chose Cheam School, which he thought would toughen up his shy, sensitive son. He wanted Charles to grow into a strong, confident young man.

Cheam School in England

The problem was that Charles was nothing like his outgoing, athletic father. He wasn't good at sports, and he didn't mix well with other boys. Charles hated Cheam. He cried himself to sleep some nights.

He didn't get any special treatment. When Charles broke the rules, he was beaten by the headmaster, like many of the other boys.

Elizabeth knew that Charles was miserable. But she decided to let Philip make all the decisions about school. It was her way of putting her husband in charge of something. In so many ways, Philip had to take a back seat to the Queen.

He was never allowed to walk in front of her. His children didn't have his family name. And he wasn't allowed to see the secret government papers in Elizabeth's red-leather boxes.

So Philip made all the rules about the children, and Elizabeth didn't argue with him.

When Charles turned thirteen, Philip sent him to an even harsher boarding school. It was the school Philip himself had attended— Gordonstoun School, in northern Scotland.

Gordonstoun School in Scotland

Philip had loved Gordonstoun when he was a young man. He didn't mind the freezing weather and icy rooms. He was proud of being able to withstand cold showers and get up for early-morning runs. But Charles hated it all. He was bullied and beaten by his roommates. He begged to return home, but Philip wouldn't let him. Charles later said it felt like a five-year "prison sentence."

Charles had one person on his side through his unhappy school years—his great-uncle Louis Mountbatten, better known as Uncle Dickie.

Dickie was like a kind grandfather. Charles felt he could talk to him without being criticized.

The Queen didn't see her children every day—but she made sure to see her dogs and horses whenever she possibly could. She had a pack of

Lord Mountbatten

corgis—sometimes as many as a dozen! They followed her around the palace and even came running in during fancy luncheons.

She also had a stable full of thoroughbred racehorses. She rode every day and made all the decisions about breeding the horses. When foals were born, she could tell them apart better than her stable hands.

Her dream was to win the most important race in England—the Epsom Derby in Surrey, better known simply as the Derby. Over the years, her horses have won big races at Ascot, a famous racetrack right down the road from Windsor Castle. But no horse of hers has ever won the Derby.

CHAPTER 7
A Busy Life

In recent years, the Queen has cut back on her schedule of events. Now that she's in her nineties, she lets Prince Charles stand in for her at some ceremonies. But throughout most of her reign, her yearly schedule was packed with events. She toured the world and hosted two state dinners

every year. She also gave garden parties every summer at Buckingham Palace. Eight thousand people were invited to each of those gatherings— teachers, firemen, soldiers, volunteers, and others. Twenty thousand sandwiches and twenty thousand slices of cake were served at each party. The garden parties were a way for the Queen to thank hardworking people for their service to England.

The Queen also performed ceremonies every year to hand out medals and titles to people. Sometimes, she "knighted" people, giving them the title of "Sir." (Women were honored as "Dames.") To be knighted, a man knelt before the Queen. Then she tapped him on both shoulders with a sword. In 1997, Paul McCartney of the Beatles was knighted.

Paul McCartney is knighted by the Queen

Other yearly events for the Queen include her birthday parade—which is *not* held on her birthday! It always takes place in June because the weather is better then. More than a thousand military men and women march through the streets in colorful uniforms. Bands play and, when she was younger, the Queen inspected the troops on horseback.

One of the fanciest and oldest events (dating back to medieval times) each year is called Garter Day. It celebrates the Knights of the Garter—the most exclusive knighthood in England. Only twenty-four people can be Garter Knights at any one time, plus several senior members of the royal family. All of them have been personally chosen by the Queen. On Garter Day, she and her knights dress in black-velvet robes and wear hats with huge white plumes on top. They walk through the streets of Windsor Castle with marching bands playing. Beginning in 1987, women could be chosen as Garter Knights.

To help the Queen organize her busy schedule, she has two private secretaries. They live in the palace and arrange every event the Queen attends. She spends so much time with them that they have become almost like close friends. The Queen doesn't have friends from the outside world. Her closest friends are mostly family members, ladies-in-waiting, and people who work in the palace.

The Queen has always kept up with whatever was new and exciting in the world. So each year, she invites ten or twelve of the smartest and most talented people in the United Kingdom to Windsor Castle. Artists, writers, professors, and others are invited to the fanciest sleepover party imaginable! The guests are treated like royalty. They have their own maids to unpack their clothes. Their bedrooms are filled with fresh flowers, candies, and fruits. The Queen wears a long gown and diamond necklace to dinner. All the guests dress up as if they're going to a ball.

Meeting people from outside the palace has been a good way for Elizabeth to keep up with a changing world. She realized long ago that if the monarchy was going to survive, the Queen herself would have to change, too.

CHAPTER 8
Changing Times

By the 1970s, many British people were getting a little tired of the monarchy. Times were hard for most people. Heating oil was so expensive, people wore coats at work on cold days. Offices were sometimes lit by candles.

Nearly half the population in Britain were so poor, they were on welfare—receiving money from the government.

The British people thought it was costing them too much money to pay for the Queen's royal lifestyle. If she was so rich, why were taxpayers giving her money every year? Many British people didn't realize that the Queen wasn't quite as rich as she seemed.

The Queen wasn't very popular during those hard years. But one member of the royal family was well liked during that era—Prince Charles. In 1970, Charles was a young, handsome prince who would be king someday. Whom would he marry? Everyone wanted to know.

Charles didn't want to choose a wife too quickly. So when he met Camilla Shand in 1970 and fell in love with her, he didn't ask her to marry him. Instead, he went off to join the Royal Navy in 1971. While he was gone,

Camilla married someone else. Charles had missed his chance!

Other changes were happening in the 1970s. For the first time in British history, a woman was elected as the prime minister in 1979. Her name was Margaret Thatcher. She was almost the same age as Queen Elizabeth.

Margaret Thatcher

Elizabeth was excited that a woman was in charge. She asked her horse trainer what he thought. His answer was surprising to hear. He said: "I'm not sure I can get my head around a woman running the country." She had to laugh, even though his comment wasn't so funny. After all, she was a woman—and she was the Queen!

But the worst, most heartbreaking changes in the 1970s had to do with Ireland.

In the 1970s, the Troubles hit close to home for Elizabeth and others when the Irish Republican Army, called the IRA, set off many bombs in London. Dozens of people were injured or killed. Even Parliament and the Tower of London were attacked. The tragedy hit the royal family hard in 1979 when a boat off the coast of Ireland was blown up. Philip's uncle Dickie Mountbatten was killed in the blast. He had been like a father to Philip and like a beloved grandfather to Prince Charles.

The whole family was devastated. Charles felt that life would never be the same. He said it would be a very long time before he could forgive "those people." But the Queen didn't harden her heart against the Irish. She never forgot that she was their queen, too.

Would the 1980s bring happier times for both the royal family and the country?

The Troubles in Ireland

The Republic of Ireland is an independent country, not part of the UK. But the country called Northern Ireland is part of the UK. Starting in the late 1960s, people in Northern Ireland fought over whether they should stay in the UK or join with Ireland in the south. Protestants wanted to stay connected to England. Catholics wanted to join the Republic of Ireland. The conflict, known as the Troubles, lasted thirty years and became violent. Many people were killed. It wasn't until 1998 that both sides agreed to stop the violence and work out their differences peacefully.

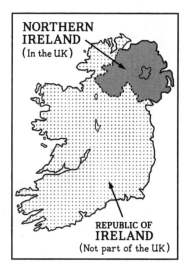

NORTHERN IRELAND (In the UK)

REPUBLIC OF IRELAND (Not part of the UK)

Who Pays the Queen?

The Queen doesn't really own most of the jewels, paintings, castles, and palaces herself. Those riches belong to the crown—to the king or queen at the time. Elizabeth can't sell the jewels or palaces, and she doesn't get any money from most of them. In 1760, King George III had agreed to give up all the income from his properties to Parliament.

King George III

In exchange, Parliament agreed to pay for the monarchy's expenses. Over the years, the cost of running a palace kept going up. The Queen often had to ask Parliament for a raise in order to pay her bills.

In 2013, Parliament changed the rules so the monarch doesn't have to ask for a raise. The king or queen gets part of the income from the properties that King George III gave up more than 250 years ago.

CHAPTER 9
Wedding for a Prince

By 1979, Charles was over thirty. He would someday be king. The Queen thought Prince Charles had waited long enough to get married.

Lady Diana Spencer was someone Charles had known for years. She seemed like a perfect match—a young, beautiful preschool teacher from a family with land and a title. And Diana had a crush on Charles.

The problem was that Charles didn't really love her. He was still in love with Camilla. Even though Camilla was married, she and Charles were still close friends. What should he do?

Finally, Prince Philip took charge. He told Charles to either marry Diana or end the relationship.

Lady Diana Spencer

So Charles proposed to Diana in February 1981. Instantly, the whole world fell in love with her. The newspapers called her Lady Di.

Photographers followed her everywhere. But Diana was shy. She hated being chased and photographed every time she left her house.

LADY DI **CHARLES**

A girl who was born to be queen

Prince who waited for true love...

Relaxed

Debutante

Local

Tradition

Serious

Growing into a royal bride

The bachelor Action Man...

Stunning

Isolated

The wedding for Charles and Diana was held on July 29, 1981. Seven hundred fifty million people around the world watched on TV. Diana wore a dress billowing with lace and ruffles. The train was twenty-five feet long. After the ceremony, she and Charles rode through London in an open horse-drawn carriage.

But was Diana happy? Not really. She felt sure that Charles was still thinking about Camilla.

Still, there were wonderful occasions. On June 21, 1982, Princess Diana gave birth to Prince William. The Queen was delighted to have a grandson and heir to the throne. Two years later, Prince Harry was born. The British liked to say that meant they had "an heir and a spare." Harry could be king if something happened to William.

Prince Andrew and Sarah Ferguson

In 1986, Elizabeth's second son, Prince Andrew, married Sarah Ferguson—a redhead with a big smile and fun-loving spirit. The newspapers called her Fergie. The British people were happy to support the monarchy again. Royal weddings and royal babies were good for the monarchy business!

CHAPTER 10
A Horrible Year, a Terrible Decade

Queen Elizabeth felt that when her uncle Edward had abdicated to marry a divorced American woman, it left a stain on the royal family. So when her children's marriages started to fall apart, she was very unhappy.

In 1992, British newspapers printed embarrassing stories about Charles and Diana. Soon, everyone found out that Charles had

cheated on Diana with Camilla. Charles and Diana's marriage was not the only troubled one. Princess Anne got divorced in 1992. Prince Andrew and Fergie separated that year and were divorced in 1996.

But the worst time for the Queen came on November 20, 1992. A fire broke out at Windsor Castle. Firefighters battled the blaze for fifteen hours. Huge portions of the castle were destroyed. Elizabeth stood in the rain, watching. Windsor is filled with priceless art. It is also the place she calls home. The fire left her more shaken up than anything else that had ever happened.

Four days later, the Queen gave a speech at an important luncheon. In her speech, Elizabeth called 1992 an *annus horribilis*—a Latin phrase meaning it was a horrible year. The speech was shown on TV. People could see how terribly upset the Queen was.

The rest of the 1990s weren't much better. In 1996, the Queen finally agreed that Charles and Diana should divorce. A year later, on August 31, 1997, Princess Diana was killed in a car crash in Paris. News photographers had been chasing her. Her chauffeur sped up to escape them but hit a tunnel wall.

THE EXPRESS
AUGUST 31, 1997 ON SUNDAY 75p
DIANA IS DEAD
6 AM NEWS SPECIAL
Princess and Dodi killed in car smash

The whole world was shocked by Diana's death. Even though she and Charles had divorced, the public continued to love and admire her.

She had become the "People's Princess," devoting much of her life to good deeds. She was the first famous person to shake hands with a patient who had AIDS and hold babies who had AIDS.

She worked to help homeless people and drug addicts. No one else in the royal family had ever done these things.

When Diana died, thousands of people showed up at Buckingham Palace. They brought flowers, notes, balloons, and stuffed animals to leave in front of the palace gates.

The British people waited for the Queen to help them grieve over the princess's death. But at first, Buckingham Palace put out only a few words about the tragedy. Days went by with nothing more from the Queen. The public began to get angry. A newspaper headline said: "Show Us You Care." Another paper wrote: "Where Is Our Queen?"

Finally, five days after Diana's death, the Queen returned to London from Scotland and made a speech on TV. Then she walked along the gates at Buckingham Palace to see all the flowers and cards. At last, the public could see that the Queen cared.

The funeral was one of the most emotional events England had ever experienced. Charles and Diana's sons—William and Harry—were only fifteen and twelve years old, respectively.

But they bravely walked behind their mother's coffin through the streets of London, with their father and grandfather at their sides. As the coffin passed by, hundreds of thousands of mourners were silent. All of London was silent except for the sound of horses' hooves—and weeping.

CHAPTER 11
A Twenty-First-Century Queen

During her reign, Queen Elizabeth has witnessed some of the most important moments in history—wars, pandemics, terrorist attacks. She doesn't have the power to change much, but she knows that the world has changed drastically during her time on the throne.

Queen Elizabeth II sending her first email, 1976

Years ago, Elizabeth decided the best thing she could do was to accept new ideas. When computers were new, she was one of the first in the palace to use them. She got an iPod at the age of seventy-nine. She has an Instagram account with a mass of followers. The palace staff post videos of the royal family so the world can see how hard everyone works.

theroyalfamily ✹

3,334
Posts

10M
Followers

36
Following

The Royal Family
Photos and videos from the work & activities of The Queen & The Royal Family.
wwwwwwwwwwwww. uu

The twenty-first century has brought new members to the royal family. Prince Charles finally married Camilla in 2005. In 2011, Prince William married Kate Middleton, a young woman he had dated all through college. They now have three children—George, Charlotte, and Louis.

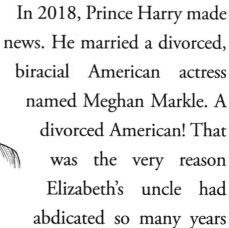

Meghan Markle

In 2018, Prince Harry made news. He married a divorced, biracial American actress named Meghan Markle. A divorced American! That was the very reason Elizabeth's uncle had abdicated so many years before. But times had changed—or at least Harry hoped so. The Queen accepted Meghan into the family. She and Harry were married in the church at Windsor Castle.

But royal life was hard for the new couple. Some newspapers ran hurtful articles about Meghan. Was this because she is  biracial, many wondered? Also, not all members of the royal family welcomed her in the way Harry had hoped. In 2020, Harry and Meghan decided to give up their royal duties and moved to the United States. This was big news around the world!

In 2021, Prince Philip died at the age of ninety-nine. His funeral—like all funerals for the royal family—had been planned years in advance. The funeral for each member of the royal family is given a code name—the name of a famous bridge. Prince Philip's funeral was code-named "Forth Bridge." For Queen Elizabeth II, the code name is "London Bridge." The moment she dies, her staff will call the prime minister to say, "London Bridge is down."

Prince Philip's funeral was very small because of the COVID-19 pandemic. Only thirty family members attended. They sat far apart from one another in the chapel at Windsor Castle. But the funeral was shown on television throughout the world. Dressed all in black, the Queen looked sad and alone, sitting by herself in the pew. Her bowed head told the world how much she grieved for the prince she had loved since she was a young girl.

Throughout her reign, Queen Elizabeth has done her best to carry on the traditions of the past. At the same time, she has embraced changes that keep the monarchy in the hearts of the British people. She has been on the throne longer than any other monarch in history.

Now that her husband is gone, she will bear her life's burdens alone. But she is prepared to do the job. No matter how the world changes around her, Queen Elizabeth II will continue to serve her country with honor, dignity, and strength.

Timeline of Queen Elizabeth II

1926 — Elizabeth Alexandra Mary Windsor is born in London

1936 — Elizabeth's uncle becomes King Edward VIII

— In December, her uncle abdicates, and her father becomes King George VI

1939 — Moves to Windsor Castle with her younger sister, Princess Margaret, during World War II

1947 — Marries Prince Philip

1948 — First child, Prince Charles, is born

1950 — Second child, Princess Anne, is born

1952 — Her father, King George VI, dies, and Elizabeth becomes queen

1953 — Coronation of Elizabeth II in Westminster Abbey

— First of many world tours to visit Commonwealth nations

1960 — Third child, Prince Andrew, is born

1981 — Prince Charles marries Lady Diana Spencer

1996 — Charles and Diana divorce

1997 — Princess Diana is killed in a car crash in Paris

2002 — Queen celebrates Golden Jubilee, fifty years on the throne

2021 — Prince Philip dies

Timeline of the World

1927	Charles Lindbergh is the first man to fly solo across the Atlantic
1939	Nazis invade Poland, starting World War II
1945	World War II ends
1957	The UK allows women to join Parliament's House of Lords for the first time
1961	US president John F. Kennedy announces the US will send a man to the moon
1963	Martin Luther King Jr. makes his famous "I Have a Dream" speech
1974	US president Richard M. Nixon resigns after impeachment hearings
1983	Sally Ride becomes the first female American astronaut in space
1989	The Berlin Wall is torn down, and the Soviet Union collapses as Communism is overthrown
1994	Nelson Mandela is elected president of South Africa
2001	The World Trade Towers are attacked on 9/11
2003	Iraq War begins
2007	First iPhone is released
2019	COVID-19 disease begins to spread around the world, starting a pandemic

Bibliography

Houston, Rob et al., editors. *Queen Elizabeth II and the Royal Family.* New York: DK Publishing, 2015.

Kelly, Angela. *The Other Side of the Coin: The Queen, the Dresser and the Wardrobe.* New York: HarperCollins, 2019.

Ryan, Catherine. *The Queen EIIR: The Life and Times of Elizabeth II.* New York: Chartwell Books, 2017.

Smith, Sally Bedell. *Elizabeth the Queen: The Life of a Modern Monarch.* New York: Random House, 2012.

Websites

https://www.rct.uk

https://www.royal.uk